latin dancing

a *flowmotion*™ title

latin dancing

dessi and orod ohanians

Created and conceived by
Axis Publishing Limited
8c Accommodation Road
London NW11 8ED
www.axispublishing.co.uk

Creative Director: Siân Keogh
Managing Editor: Brian Burns
Project Designer: Sean Keogh
Project Editor: Antony Atha
Production Manager: Sue Bayliss
Photographer: Mike Good

Library of Congress Cataloging-in-Publication
Data Available

10 9 8 7 6 5 4 3 2 1

Published in 2002 by Sterling Publishing Co., Inc.
387 Park Avenue South, New York, NY 10016
Text and images © Axis Publishing Limited 2002
Distributed in Canada by Sterling Publishing
C/o Canadian Manda Group,
One Atlantic Avenue, Suite 105
Toronto, Ontario, M6K 3E7, Canada

Separation by
United Graphics Pte Limited
Printed and bound by
Star Standard (Pte) Limited

Sterling ISBN 0–8069–9381–2

a *flowmotion*™ title

latin dancing

contents

introduction

Salsa, merengue, lambada—these three dances are the soul and culture of Latin America, dances that the whole world has come to enjoy more and more over the past decade. Each dance comes from a different country and culture, and each has its own history and rhythm. What links them is the energy and passion for life present in their music, the romance of partners dancing in harmony, and the way the dances bring people together.

In this book we present a quick introduction to these three dances—the Cuban salsa, the Brazilian lambada, and the merengue from the Dominican Republic. The dances are often referred to as "street" dances. They were, and are, danced by ordinary people in their everyday lives, not only in clubs but often just on the streets. There are very few hard and fast rules about how to perform these dances: all can be interpreted freely, and each dancer can demonstrate their own personality in the dance. More complicated steps are always being added to make the dances challenging to dance and spectacular to watch. You can dance, making each step and move technically correct, or dance as spontaneously as you like. The most important thing is to remember to enjoy yourself.

There are, however, some basic principles that every Latin dancer needs to follow:

● Never use the same foot twice in a row—step on the right foot have to be followed by a step on the left

● Dance mirror image to your partner—left foot for one partner means right foot to the other

● Transfer weight from foot to foot as you mark the beat—the body sways from foot to foot as the steps are executed.

Each dance has its own steps, sequences, and movements. However, it is not important to know millions of combinations—just dance with passion and enthusiasm. Let the music move your feet and body. In this book, you will find pointers to good dance posture, and the holds and hip movements for each dance. The routines shown can be put together and carried out as a complete dance, but feel free to improvise and experiment.

salsa

There are many opinions over when salsa was created, or indeed where it came from—Cuba, Puerto Rico, or Colombia. Only one thing is known for sure—salsa is a melting pot of many Latin and Afro-Caribbean dances; each of them played an important part in its creation.

A lot of people believe that salsa originated in Cuba. It may be so, but no one can prove it for certain. Danzón was cetainly one of the main contributors, but other steps were borrowed from the rumba of Africa, together with cumbia, guaguanco, guajira, Cuban son, mambo, montuno, cha-cha-cha, and various Spanish rhythms as the music developed. Traditional salsa music was played on a clave (an instrument in the shape of two round wooden sticks that hit into each other).

At the same time salsa was adopted in other countries such as the Dominican Republic, Colombi, and Puerto Rico. Later, the musicians took the rhythms to the USA and Mexico, as these spread from New York to Miami. The New Yorkans created the word "salsa" to describe the music, to help to make it a commercial success. The music then started to be broadcast on TV and radio, and attracted a number of composers.

In modern salsa, you can hear the influence of son and cumbia, even, in some cases, mixtures of guaracha and merengue. In the past 30 years salsa has evolved in many ways—not only in the way people dance it, but in the way that the music is played, to provide a variety of rhythms. For instance the different style of salsa that has been developed in New York has led to the use of the instruments with an extra percussion. New Yorkers, who dance mambo (on the beat two), could comfortably dance to the rhythm and beat of salsa derived from son, while dancers in Miami and Los Angeles adapted the Cuban style of dancing (on beat one).

In some ways salsa is quite close to the mambo. The steps are danced on eight counts of music, and the moves and patterns are often similar. However, salsa has many turns that are different from mambo, and is more of a side-to-side dance.

Salsa is most important in the music industry. It has many roots, but everyone agrees that the music is hugely exciting and has attracted a worldwide following. No one method of dancing salsa is the best; technical excellence, smoothness, and style are all very well; but the most important thing is the feeling that you bring to dancing with your partner. The romance and the passion of the dance between partners take precedence over everything else.

basis for the moves and signalling

As we have seen, salsa originated as a street dance. It was, therefore, not very structured, and had few set moves. In this book we have taken the dance apart to simplify and improve the techniques. We have created a set of signals, steps, and styling for both men and women, from basic steps for beginners, to intricate moves and drops for master dancers. The advanced techniques are designed to allow everyone to dance with elegance and precision.

Each step in salsa consists of four beats. In Cuban salsa, we do a light touch to the floor with the toe on the first beat, which is called a "tap." Next, we step with the same foot one way or another (depending on the step), straightening the knee as we transfer the weight, and lifting the stationary foot. On the third beat, we move the weight back to the center; and, on the fourth count, we bring the feet together. Then, the same pattern is repeated on the other leg. As we transfer weight on the moving foot, we need to exaggerate the step by moving our hips in the same direction This is what gives the general look of the dance.

Salsa steps take place on eight beats of music. The way we dance salsa count 1 of the music is the tap; the first step of the dance comes on count 2. When we step, we call that a break. We call this dancing "on two." This is when we take the first step, on the second count of the music (mambo is also danced in this manner). Cuban salsa differs from this, and is called dancing "on one" because the step is taken on the first count of the music.

There are two ways we hold each other while dancing: a close hold is when the leader's left hand is holding the follower's right hand; the leader's right hand is at the base of the spine of the follower, and the follower's left

CLOSE HOLD   **OPEN HOLD**

hand is on the shoulder of the leader. In this position, the leader stands slightly to the left of his partner, so that their knees are not directly opposite, and pass each other as they bend.

In the open hold, partners hold each other by the hands, standing directly in front of each other about one foot's distance apart. This is the position from which most of the sequences begin, and is used particularly for spins and turns.

During the dance, the dancers seldom speak to each other. So how does the leader tell the follower what to do? This is very simple. The way the leader holds the follower will give her an indication of what is going to happen. We call this "giving a signal," and these are shown in detail in the dance sequences. The signals are very simple—simply changing the hand position indicates a change in step. The signals are not the same for all moves, and follow from the most comfortable handhold for each move. For example, when giving the signal for a spin, the leader moves his fingers from underneath the follower's hand to the top. He then has a comfortable grip to give her support during spin. Signals are important to make your dance easy and flowing. Everyone wants to dance in harmony with their partner, not fight with them on the dance floor.

It is good practice to stand up straight while you dance. Slouching might make you look lazy. Keep the steps small—there may well be someone behind you on the dance floor. This also helps you keep up with fast music. Try to look at your partner from time to time and, most importantly, encourage your partner with a smile.

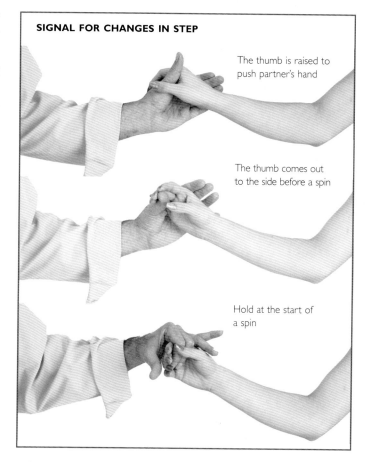

SIGNAL FOR CHANGES IN STEP

The thumb is raised to push partner's hand

The thumb comes out to the side before a spin

Hold at the start of a spin

lambada

Lambada was once called the forbidden dance. This came from the "dança da garrafa," a dance in which a woman danced, crouching down over a standing-up bottle, trying to get as close as she could to the top without touching it.

This dance is seldom found today, but lambada, with its hot and spicy rhythm, is one of the most sensual and romantic forms of dance that has ever been created. You cannot help but feel drawn to it once you have tried it.

Lambada originated in the small bars and cafés of Brazil, called lambaterias, where people used to dance, entwined together. This eventually became lambada as we know it today.

It is popularly supposed that lambada was an offspring of dances such as carimbo and merengue, with influences drawn from forro and samba. Undoubtedly, lambada was influenced by Caribbean music. But the music is a combination of Caribbean drums, metallic, and electric guitars, with an added touch of Spanish and local Indian flavours making up the final dance.

Lambada travelled from Brazil to Bahia, where it evolved and developed, particularly in Porto Seguro, where people danced lambada on their toes, with their legs arched. It was also fashionable to dance in flared skirts and extremely close to one another. People in the south-east region of Brazil disliked these rhythms, which came from Bahia.

In its original form, lambada lasted only a very short time in Brazil. It really took off in 1989, when a French band called Kaoma brought the dance to Europe and marketed it in a fresh way. Lambada took Europe by storm. The timing was perfect. For the first time since the sixties, here was music to encourage couples to dance in a romantic embrace. The European influence was so powerful that Brazil again took lambada to its heart. Lambada music spread from Europe to Japan, the USA, and the Middle East. It created a new excitement in the dance world. In turn, their Brazilian singers, such as Fafa do Belem, Daniela Mercury, and many more, started to make lambada music. The craze was unstoppable.

There wasn't enough music around so people started

to find substitute music with the characteristic three-beat rhythm—music such as zuke, Arabic, and Turkish music, and, most popular of all, Gypsy Kings and Spanish rumbas.

Today, you can dance lambada in crowded nightclubs and dance clubs, and, in the past few years, lambada routines have evolved to include a mixture of jive spins, merengue, rumba, and even Sevillianas. Some very acrobatic moves have also been added.

steps and moves

Lambada music is a three beat music with the clear count of quick—quick—slow. The first beat of the music is stepped on the spot, the second is generally a movement in one direction or another, and the third is a transfer of weight back to the center, this time on the slow beat, with a slower movement of the leg. Lambada is danced with the whole body—not just with the lower part, as is salsa. The dancers, especially the women, should dance on their toes. The origin of this is that lambada was first danced barefoot on the beaches of Brazil, where the sand is so hot that dancers could not step on it with their whole foot. Knees should be slightly bent, and stay bent and supple even when the weight is transferred from one foot to the other. The upper body moves in the opposite direction to the lower—generally if the hips are twisted in one direction, the rib cage is twisted in the opposite direction. This becomes more exaggerated and when the dancers are more experienced. Lambada is danced very, very close. The dancers should appear to be almost glued to each other. In that way, partners can create an image of moving together as one.

To be a good leader in lambada, the man needs to imagine that the woman is a piece of clay in his hands that can be molded by pressing and manipulating to create the perfect shape. That is why lambada has no signals, for the woman should be completely relaxed, and allow her partner to put her into the right position.

In lambada, women have the opportunity to "decorate" the dance with head movements. These are completely optional. It is the woman's choice how much or how little to do.

When attempting the dips, start these as a wave from the knees upward through the hips, and shoulders, with your head movement last. Don't be too ambitious: only do as much as fitness permits.

merengue

There are many different type of merengue music. Some are fast, some slow, and it can be played on different instruments. Tempos vary a great deal, from slow to fast, quickening in pace toward the latter part of the dance. The slow merengue, resembling bolero, seems to be more popular in clubs and restaurants running dance nights, and today often resembles jive in its closing stages.

The merengue is the national dance of the Dominican Republic, and is hugely popular throughout the Caribbean, in Haiti, and the neighboring islands.

There are many claims as to the origins of merengue. One such claim is that, in the early 1800s, African slaves on the plantations mimicked the ballroom dances held in the big estate houses owned by the Europeans planters. When they had their own festivities, they recreated these in the barns. To make the dance more fun, over time, the slaves added a special beat of the drums to add more rhythm to their dance.

Originally, merengue was not danced by couples, but in a circle, each man and woman facing each other, holding hands at arm's length. They did not dance as closely as today. The majority of dances that originated in Africa—and there are many throughout the world—share the common feature of being dominated by steps and arm movements. The original movements were mainly the shaking of the shoulders and swift movement of the feet. Unlike today, there was little hip movement, for the native African dancers did not move their hips.

Merengue has been very popular in the Dominican Republic since the 19th century. Not only was it danced at every celebration and special occasion throughout the country, but it spread from there to become popular throughout the Caribbean.

At the beginning of the 20th century, some educated musicians organized a big campaign to introduce this dance into the ballrooms. Popular musicians joined the campaign, but always met resistance because the original tunes were accompanied by very vulgar lyrics. Juan F. García, Juan Espínola, and Julio Alberto Hernandez were the first to try to change the image of merengue. They had little success to start with, for polite society refused to accept merengue, even though the musicians themselves were well established and extremely popular.

It was not until an aristocratic family from Santiago asked Luis Alberti to write a merengue song with "decent lyrics," to mark their daughter's fifteenth birthday celebrations, that merengue was accepted. The song became a hit, and is thought of today as a sort of anthem for the merengue. From then on, merengue became very popular, especially when it started being broadcast on the radio.

Popular musicians tried to imitate and follow the model created by these first musicians, while in the country, the musicians continued playing merengue the traditional way. This produced two very different types of merengue: folklore merengue, which can still be found in the countryside; and ballroom merengue, which is the most commonly known.

In the Dominican Republic, merengue experienced a golden age during the dictatorship of Rafael Trujillo, from the 1930s until his assassination in 1961. Trujillo was from peasant stock, and he promoted the music as a symbol of national expression and the culture of the former underclass.

The close hold for dancing the merengue. The man's hand is at the base of his partner's spine.

moves and combinations

The basis of modern merengue is a transfer of weight from one foot to the other, combined with exaggerated hip movements. The upper body stays relatively relaxed. There are many hand changes by women going around the men or vice versa.

Merengue has distinct moves of its own that do not originate in salsa as many believe. In most salsa clubs these days, merengue is danced in between salsa dances to add variety. There is a lot of opportunity to experiment and create interesting moves of your own, because the steps are so simple. Nowadays, merengue is a hugely popular dance all over the Caribbean and Latin America, and has become well known throuughout the USA. It can be danced by anyone—even someone with no previous dance experience. Merengue music is very lively and is bound to add a Latin American feel to any party.

Merengue relies on exaggerated hip movement for its appeal.

The hips move to the side as the dancers transfer their weight.

go with the flow

The special *Flowmotion* images used in this book have been created to ensure you see the whole of each dance sequence—not just selected highlights. Each sequence is labelled suitable for beginners or intermediate dancers by a coloured tab above the title. The captions along the bottom of the images provide additional information to help you perform the steps confidently. Below this, another layer of information shows how the steps are taken on each beat of the bar. The photographs in bold show the position "on the beat," which helps beginners to visualize each step. In most Latin American dances, dancers move one way to start with, and then return, stepping in the opposite direction.

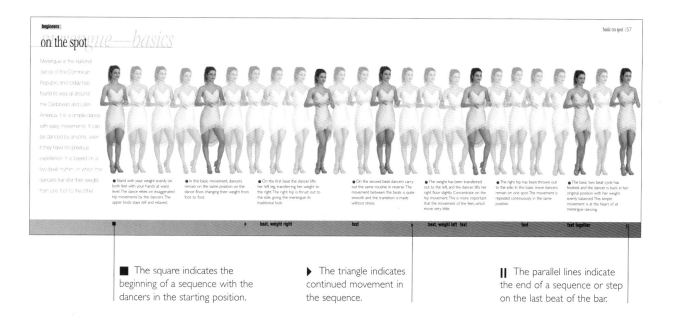

■ The square indicates the beginning of a sequence with the dancers in the starting position.

▶ The triangle indicates continued movement in the sequence.

‖ The parallel lines indicate the end of a sequence or step on the last beat of the bar.

salsa

forward and back step

The basic steps of salsa are simple, but the accent is on the style. This shows the forward and back movement. The steps of all the basic moves are the same both for the man and woman.

● Stand with your feet together, then transfer your weight on to the ball of your right foot. Lift your knee with your toe pointing to the ground and tap your left toe lightly on the first beat of the music.

● The forward step is made with your left foot in time with the music and is quite small; the first moves are just the introduction to the dance. As the step proceeds, transfer your weight forward on to your left foot.

● Your hip follows the direction of the step. This gives the step the authentic salsa style. On the third beat transfer your weight back on to your right foot. This should be in the place where you started.

● On the fourth beat the feet come together, the complete step goes: beat, tap, beat forward, beat, back, beat together.

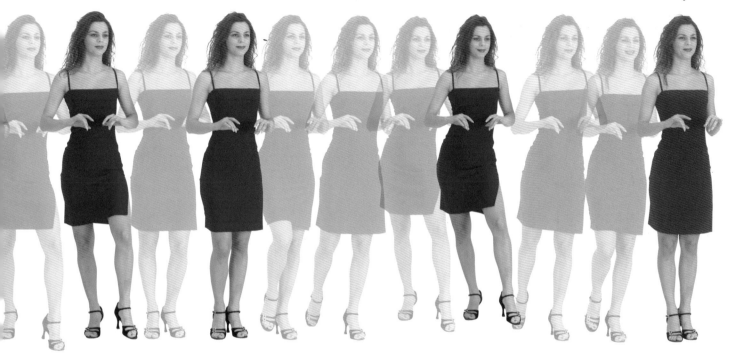

● The step is now repeated in the opposite direction with the tap and step back being made with the right foot. The complete step goes: beat, tap, beat, back, beat, forward, beat together.

● On the back step move your weight back on to your right heel. The right hip is thrown out to the side. Your feet should skim the floor and the transference of weight is always controlled by your knee and ankle.

● Push your weight down on to your foot and keep your upper body still. Imagine that you are meeting some resistance from the floor. On the last beat bring your left leg back level with your right to the starting position.

● This first basic move is included in many salsa routines. It is danced in exactly the same both by the man and woman. When danced with a partner, the movements of the man and woman mirror each other.

▶ **beat, tap**   ▶ **beat, back**   ▶ **beat, forward**   ▶ **beat, together**   **II**

step back and back*ic steps*

salsa basic steps

The second basic salsa step is an extension of the first; in this step the first movement after the tap is backward. As the name implies there are two steps, first with the left foot, then with the right.

● Start the move in the normal way by making a tap with your left foot on the first beat of the music. The tap should be made with the ball of your left foot touching the floor lightly. Your weight is on your right foot.

● On the second beat of the music, take a small step backward with your left foot. At this stage your weight is still on your right foot with your hip to the right.

● On the third beat the weight comes forward on to the right foot. Remember to keep your body still with all your movement taking place from the waist downward. This is the essence of correct salsa dancing.

● On the fourth beat the feet come together back in the starting position. The complete step goes: beat, tap, beat back, beat forward, beat together.

● On the first beat of the next bar the tap is made, this time with the right foot. Keep your toe pointing downward to the ground.

● On the second beat the step is made backward, this time with the right foot. Your weight is on the left with the left hip out to the side.

● On the third beat of the music your weight comes forward again on to your left foot and on the fourth beat you bring your feet together.

● This completes the movement. Your feet are now together at the starting position, ready to make the next move in the dance. Remember, all the movement comes from the waist downward.

▶ **beat, tap**   ▶ **beat, step back**   ▶ **beat, forward**   ▶ **beat, together**   II

opening up *basic steps*

Making stylish turns is one of the beauties of salsa. Opening up is the first move in making a turn and is shown here with the man and woman moving around 180° and then back again. There are four beats for each sequence, and the build up to the movement should occur naturally, taking its rhythm from the dance itself.

● Start in the usual salsa position, and on the first beat on the music make a light tap with your left foot. Keeping your weight on your right foot, take a small step back on to your left foot on the second beat.

● This is the start of the turn, or opening up. You need to have your weight further back than usual to allow your body to swing around, pivoting on the ball of your right foot.

● On the third beat move your left foot around your right, swinging your body in a 180° turn. You will need to keep your left knee slightly bent while you make this move to allow you to pivot freely into the finishing position.

▶ **beat, tap**　　　▶ **beat, step**　　　▶ **beat, swing**　　　▶

● On the fourth beat transfer your weight on to the ball of your left foot, and bring your feet together to complete the movement. You are now facing the opposite way to when you started.

● To return to the starting position, repeat the sequence in reverse. This time make the tap on beat one and the first step back, on beat two, with your right foot.

● With your weight on the ball of your left foot swing your body around on the third beat. This movement has to be made quite quickly to allow you to change your body position.

● Bring your right foot up to your left to complete the turn. You are now back in the starting position ready to continue the dance.

side step — *basic steps*

The side step is found in many salsa routines. The principle is the same basic forward and step, with four beats to the sequence.

● Stand with your feet together, and on the first beat of the music, make a light tap with the ball of your left foot in the normal way. Keep your weight on your right foot with your right knee straight.

● Keeping your weight on your right leg, take a small step to the left on the second beat of the music. Your knee should be bent, with your toe pointing downward toward the floor.

● On the third beat your weight comes over on to your left leg; then lift your right leg across. Note the bent knee position, with the right foot pointing down. It takes some practice to perfect this movement.

● On the fourth beat bring your feet together, ready for the next bar. Remember to keep your upper body still; your hips should follow your movement.

● The steps are then repeated in the opposite direction. This time the tap and first step are made with your right foot.

● Make the sideways step small, and change weight easily, keeping your upper body still. On the third beat transfer your weight on to your right leg. Straighten your right knee.

● On the fourth beat move your left leg back to your right, and bring your feet together. This completes the sequence and you are now back in the starting position.

● This basic step follows exactly the same pattern as the basic forward and back sequence, but moving in a sideways direction. When danced with a partner the man and woman's steps mirror each other.

▶ **beat, tap**   ▶ **beat, step**   ▶ **beat, across**   ▶ **beat, together**   ‖

the spin
salsa—basic steps

The spin is the last basic move that salsa dancers should master before taking their partners. It is more fluid than the other basic routines and requires force to rotate the body through 360°.

● Take up the normal salsa position. On the first beat you make a tap to start the movement. This time the tap is made with your right foot not the left. The left leg is straight and the right foot is pointing down toward the floor.

● Keep your weight on your left leg, and on the second beat move your right leg out as shown, taking a small step to the right.

● When you have taken this step, move your weight out to the right and stand on your left toe. This will give you the correct leverage to push around 360°, pivoting on the ball of your left foot.

beat, tap ▶ **beat, step** ▶

● On the third beat push around into the spin. You will need to practice this movement before you can do it stylishly: it needs a good deal of control if you are to remain balanced with your left foot on one spot.

● Here the dancer is starting her rotation through 360°. You will need to keep your left leg flexible and use your hands for balance as you swing around with your right leg.

● As the spin ends, bring your right foot around so that it is pointing in the direction you started from. This movement is quite fast.

● On the fourth beat the spin is completed, and you bring your feet together into the starting position. You need to keep your body as upright and still as possible when carrying out the spin.

partners—forward and back

Once the basic salsa moves have been mastered, it is time to put them into practice with your partner. The more you dance with one person and the more you understand the moods and feelings of each dance, the better the partnership will be.

● At the start of the dance take your partner in a close hold and stand facing each other. On the first beat each person taps, the man with his left foot and the woman with her right.

● When the tap is made, both dancers lift their knees with the woman's inside the man's feet, pointing down toward the ground. On the second beat the man takes a step forward and the woman a step back.

● As the step is completed, the man's weight moves on to his left foot and the woman's to her right. Both dancers move together, keeping their upper bodies still.

● On the third beat the man takes a small step back to his original position and the woman moves forward at the same time. Their weight is transferred to the right and left legs respectively, as shown in the sequence.

● On the fourth beat the dancers bring their feet together. The step is then repeated, but this time the moves are made the other way around with the man stepping back and the woman moving forward.

● On the first beat the man taps with his right leg and the woman taps with her left. The woman's knee is outside the man's and the feet are pointing to the ground.

● On the second beat the man moves back, transferring his weight to his right leg; and at the same time the woman steps forward on to her left leg.

● On the third beat the man's weight is transferred forward on to his left leg and the woman's back to her right. On the fourth beat both dancers bring their legs together and the forward and back movement is completed.

beat, together ❙❙ ▶ **beat, tap** ▶ **beat, step** ▶ **beat, step, beat, together** ❙❙

signal to change to second basic step

When changing steps the partners need to exchange signals. This is usually given by the man and followed by the woman. This sequence shows the signals given to change from the basic forward and back step to the back and back step.

● The dancers are in the normal position, and on the first beat, the tap is made with the left and right feet of the man and woman respectively.

● On the second beat the woman steps back, as in the forward and back movement, but the man changes his footwork and steps back instead of forward.

● This moves the dancers apart. The man continues to hold the woman around the waist with his right hand, but pushes with his left hand. At the same time the woman straightens her right arm.

● On the third beat the dancers transfer their weight back to their right and left legs respectively. This brings them close together again.

■　▶　**beat, tap**　▶　**beat, step**　▶　**beat, step**　▶

● On the fourth beat both dancers bring their feet together, and the tap is made on the first beat of the following bar. The man taps with his right foot and the woman with her left.

● On the second beat the man takes a step backward with his right leg and the woman steps back with her left.

● As the couple transfers their weight on to their back foot, the man releases his hold on the woman's waist and the couple holds hands as they move apart as shown. On the third beat the couple transfers their weight back.

● The weight of the dancers is now on their front feet. On the fourth beat they bring their feet together and stand close together, facing each other holding hands.

partners—second basic step

This move is the next development where the dancers move apart, together, and apart again—first with left foot for the man and then with the right. The woman follows with the opposite legs. This movement is a good example of the rhythm and excitement of salsa as the dancers break apart and then come together again as the dance progresses.

● Stand facing each other close together. The couple holds hands throughout this movement with their elbows bent at the beginning. On the first beat the man taps with his left foot and the woman with her right.

● On the second beat each dancer takes a small step backward, away from each other, moving the left and right leg respectively. Their weight remains on the other leg.

● As the dancers' weight moves on to their back legs, they both extend their arms. The man raises his right foot off the floor and the woman her left.

● On the third beat, the dancers transfer their weight back on to their front legs. They have quarrelled, parted, and are returning to each other again.

■　　　　　　　▶　　**beat, tap**　　　　　▶　　　　**beat, step**　　　　▶　　**beat, transfer**　　　　　▶

● On the fourth beat each dancer brings their legs together and they are back in their original position, close together. The move is then repeated on the opposite side.

● On the first beat the man taps with his right foot and the woman with her left. The position is the same as before.

● On the second beat the dancers step backward, shifting their weight from their front to their back legs, and raising their front feet as shown. It is important to keep the upper body as still as possible.

● On the third beat the dancers transfer their weight back on to their front feet, and on the fourth they bring their legs together and resume the original position.

signal to change to third basic step

Turns and spins are an essential part of salsa, and all couples love to include these moves in their routines. This sequence shows the signals given when the couple wants to progress from back and back, the second basic move, to opening up, the third. The couple turns inward at the same time and then change hands to turn through 180°.

● The couple is dancing the second basic step, back and back. Start facing each other, holding hands, and tap on the first beat of the music—the man taps with his left foot, and the woman with her right.

● On the second beat both dancers take a step backward—the man with his left foot, the woman with her right. This follows the basic routine for this step with the dancers' weight on the back foot.

● At this stage in the movement, the couple is still holding hands. On the third beat the couple lets go with the right and left hand respectively, and turn inward as they transfer their weight on to their front feet.

● The turning movement should be smooth and stylish. Both dancers should move at the same time, pivoting around on the ball of their front feet.

■   ▶ **beat, tap**   ▶ **beat, step**   ▶ **beat, turn** ▶ **beat, together**

● On the fourth beat the dancers bring their inner legs together and stand side by side, each having turned through 90°. Then on beat one of the next sequence, both dancers tap with the outside foot as shown.

● On beat two, both man and woman take a step back with the outside foot. This step needs to be slightly to the side to allow the dancers space to turn toward each other, through 180°, on the next beat.

● On the third beat the dancers move their weight back on to their front feet and turn toward each other through 180°, changing hands as they do so.

● On the fourth beat they bring their feet together to finish. The movement is now complete and the dancers are again side by side, holding hands, and facing the front.

partners—third basic step

The dancers can then continue dancing the opening out move, the third basic salsa routine. Here all the turns are made through 180°. Repeated movements are an integral part of salsa and help to build up a rhythm. If you practice with one partner, you can anticipate each change so that your movements seem to flow effortlessly, one into another.

● The dancers are standing side by side holding hands. It is important to stand a reasonable distance apart to allow you to turn toward each other at the same time.

● The tap on the first beat on the music and the step backward on the second are both made with the outside foot. The tap is made lightly with the ball of the foot.

● On the second beat step backward, transferring your weight on to your outside leg. This should be straight, and as the inside leg comes up, it throws the hips out in the true salsa style.

● On the third beat move your weight back on to your front foot and swing in toward your partner, changing hands as you come face to face. It is important that the man takes the woman's hand from underneath.

● The turn continues through 180° until the couple is facing in the opposite direction. On the fourth beat they bring their legs together to complete the movement.

● The opening out movement is then repeated. Tap with your outside foot on the first beat in the bar—all the movements should flow smoothly one into the other.

● On beat two step backward with your outside foot, straighten the back leg, and then transfer you weight forward on to your front inside leg as shown. Keep you upper body as still as possible throughout.

● On beat three turn inward through 180°, changing hands in exactly the same way as before, and on the last beat bring your legs together, facing the front.

eat, together   ❙❙   **beat, tap**   ▶   **beat, step**   ▶   **beat, swing, beat, together**   ❙❙

signal to spin *salsa partners*

Spins are among the most exotic parts of salsa, and, as they are the most difficult moves to bring off with style and accuracy, both dancers have to be well prepared. It is a good idea to practice these moves. The signal to spin is given when the man changes his hold while dancing the second basic back and back move shown on pages 33–34.

● The dancers face each other, holding hands in the normal way, dancing the second basic back and back move.

● On the first beat of the bar, the dancers tap with their opposite feet as shown—the man taps with his left foot and the woman with her right.

● On the second beat both dancers move backward, away from each other, holding out their arms but keeping hold with both hands.

● On the third beat the dancers transfer their weight back on to their front legs and come close together again. At this point the man changes his grip and slides his index fingers into the girl's palm.

■   ▶   **beat, tap**   ▶   **beat, step**   ▶   **beat, transfer**   ▶

● The girl holds the man's index and middle fingers between her thumb and index finger. The whole transition is done between beats three and four when the dancers bring their legs together, facing each other.

● The dancers can then proceed to the next stage. On the first beat of the second bar, the man taps with his right foot and the girl taps with her left in the normal way.

● On the second beat both dancers step back, this time letting go with the inside hands. The man holds the girl with his left hand in her right, allowing them to sway further apart.

● On the third beat they transfer their weight on to their front feet, and on the fourth come close together. The man raises his left hand to shoulder level. The spin takes place in the next bar of the music.

change grip, together ‖ **beat, tap** ▶ **beat, step, release** ▶ **beat, transfer, beat, together** ‖

spin and side step

In this routine the girl spins from right to left, and left to right, while the man does the side step. The dance may originate as a variation on the basic theme from Latin America, but in some ways it is reminiscent of a courtly saraband with the maiden pirouetting to woo her lover, turning away and back again.

● Stand facing each other. The man's index finger is held between the thumb and forefinger of his partner. Tap on the first beat of the music– the tap is made on the side where the couple hold hands.

● On the second beat, take a step to the side. The girl moves to her right and the man to his left. The man raises his arm above shoulder level to allow his partner to spin around underneath and to the side.

● On the third beat the girl starts the spin, transferring her weight on to her left leg and pushing around with her right. Her partner holds her steady.

● The rotation should be easy and steady and flow, as if the whole movement was automatic. It takes practice to make the whole spin in one beat, and the spin must be fast, which adds to its excitement.

■ **beat, tap** ▶ **beat, step** ▶ **beat, spin** ▶ ▶

● The spin is nearly finished. On the fourth beat of the music the dancers face each other again and bring their feet together. The man drops his hand as the spin is completed, bringing his left foot back to his right.

● The next spin is made the other way, spinning from left to right, while the side step is done with the opposite foot. Tap on the first beat— the man taps with his right foot and the woman with her left.

● The dancers take a small step to the side on the second beat of the music. On the third beat the girl starts her spin as before, spinning in the other direction. The handhold remains the same throughout.

● The spin is now completed, and on the fourth beat the dancers bring their feet together Dancers perform an odd number of spins, 1, 3, or 5. This leads directly to the signal to stop spinning shown on pages 42–43.

beat, together ❙❙ **beat, tap** ▶ **beat, step, beat, spin** ▶ **beat, together** ❙❙

signal to stop spinning and come together

This sequence shows the signal for the dancers to change from the spin, back to the first basic

step. It is made by the man moving his left hand downward toward his partner's left hip.

● The dancers face each other, holding each other in a single handhold as they would if they were dancing a spin cycle.

● On the first beat the man makes the tap with his right foot and the woman with her left.

● On the second beat both dancers take a step back, but instead of raising his arm to shoulder level, the man now drops it in the direction of his partner's left hip.

● Both dancers transfer their weight on to the back leg, which should be straight. The front leg is lifted, and on the third beat their weight is transferred back to the front, bringing the dancers close together.

● On the fourth beat the dancers bring their feet together and stand facing each other, holding each other in the close contact hold.

● The finishing moves of this cycle in salsa are more spectacular. The tap is omitted, and the first and second beats are danced as one. The man takes a step forward with his left foot and the woman one back with her right.

● The couple interlock their knees and the man drops down, bending both knees, holding the woman firmly around the waist. Dancers can rotate their hips slightly, the woman to the right, the man to the left.

● On the third beat the couple resumes the upright position. At the same time, they transfer their weight on to their back feet and on the fourth beat bring their feet together, holding each other closely.

beat, together   ‖   beat, step, drop down   ▶   beat, stand up   ▶   beat, together   ‖

opening up partners

Opening out is another way of changing positions while dancing salsa. It is quite difficult to master, and you an your partner will need to practice before you can do it perfectly and with style. There are a number of side by side movements that can be incorporated in a salsa cycle, and you need to master the opening out movement before you can attempt them.

● The dancers face each other holding hands. On the first beat the man taps with his right foot and the woman with her left.

● The dancers have their weight on the other leg, and on the second beat each takes a step backward.

● As they move apart, the man lets go with his right hand. The dancers transfer their weight on to their back legs, and the man drops his hand, aiming it inward toward the woman's left hip. This signals the turn.

● On the third beat the man pulls his left hand toward him and brings it round in a semi-circle across his front, aiming it at the woman's right hip. In this way he signals to his partner to open up.

● On the fourth beat the dancers transfer their weight back on to their front legs and come together, turning to face the front. The man's right hand goes around the woman's waist.

● The next movement starts with the tap being made with the outside foot. The dancers stand at 90° to each other. On the second beat the woman takes a step back on to her right foot; the man steps to the side to his left.

● On the third beat the woman swings inward through 180°, pivoting on her left foot. The woman's arm goes around the man's back, and his left arm goes around her waist.

● On the final beat the dancers come together with the woman on the man's left, facing in the opposite direction with her arm on his shoulder. This movement can be repeated from one side to the other side.

beat, together   ❙❙   **beat, tap**   ▶   **beat, beat, turn**   ▶   **beat, together**   ❙❙

alternate spins _partners_

This is the next sequence and follows from the opening up routine shown on pages 44–45. Both dancers spin through 360°, first the man, and then the woman. As both spins take place one after another within two bars of music, it generates both movement and excitement. You will need to practice this routine with your partner to get the timing exact.

● The dancers start from the finishing position, shown on page 46, with the woman on the left. On the first beat the woman taps with her left foot and the man with his right.

● On the second beat the man transfers his weight to the right. The woman steps back leaving only the toe of her left foot on the floor.

● On the third beat the man spins 360° counterclockwise while the woman transfers her weight on to her right foot and spins 90° clockwise.

● In this bar the dancers spin separately and there is no contact between them. On the fourth beat the spins finish and the dancers come together, facing each other. The man takes hold of the woman's right hand.

■ ▶ **beat, tap, beat step** ▶ **beat, spin** ▶ **beat, together** ▶

● In the next bar the man spins the woman but does not spin himself. On the first beat the man taps with his right foot and the woman with her left in the normal way.

● On the second beat the man steps to the left while the woman transfers her weight on to her right leg, preparing o spin.

● On the third beat the woman spins around from left to right, and the man raises his hands to let her spin and provide balance. The handhold must be flexible, as the grip changes during the circle.

● On the fourth beat of the bar the spin is completed and the dancers are back in their starting positions, facing each other.

‖ **beat, tap** ▶ **beat, step** ▶ **beat, spin** ▶ **beat, together** ‖

shoulder spin *partners*

As the dance develops, the number of different spins increases. The shoulder spin is an easy variation, where the dancers remain in close contact during the move. It starts with a different hold, the cross-hold, where the man and woman hold each other with their right hands. It conveys an atmosphere of intimacy.

● The dancers hold each other, right hand to right hand. The man's index finger is held between the woman's index finger and thumb. On the first beat the man taps with his left foot, and the woman with her right.

● On the second beat the man signals by pushing his hand at shoulder level to his left, stepping to his left. The woman matches him, stepping to her right, and turns her left foot to enable her to spin around it.

● On the third beat the man brings his hand back to his right and the woman spins through 270°. The woman raises her left arm against her partner's chest and leans against his arm to stop herself from overspinning.

● On the fourth beat the dancers end up side by side, facing the front. The man's hand goes around her shoulders, and the hold is maintained throughout.

● On the next beat the man and woman tap with their right and left feet respectively, preparing to return to their starting position.

● On the second beat the man steps back on his right foot and the woman steps back on her left, preparing to spin around on her right foot.

● On the third beat the man raises his arm and pulls the woman toward him, spinning her in a clockwise direction. Again the turn is made through 270° with the man leading the woman as shown.

● The turn is completed, and on the fourth beat the partners are back in the starting position, facing each other.

▶ **beat, tap** ▶ **beat, step** ▶ **beat, spin** ▶ **beat, together** ‖

wrapping spin *partners*

The movements of the waist spin are very similar to the shoulder spin, and the signal to spin is given in the same way. The only difference is that the man keeps his hands at waist level and does not raise it to shoulder height. Both spins are essential in a varied salsa routine.

● Face each other, holding right hand to right hand, with the man's index finger held between the thumb and forefinger of the woman's hand. On the first beat, tap—the man with his left foot, the woman with her right.

● On the second beat the man steps to the side on his left, the woman to the right, transferring her weight on to her left foot, preparing for the spin.

● On the third beat the man pushes his hand back, across to his left, and spins the woman around on her left foot. The dancers maintain their handhold, and the man's hand goes around the woman's waist.

● On the fourth beat the dancers come close together. The woman's arm goes across her back, and the man holds her hand at waist level.

● On the first beat of the next bar, the dancers tap, the man with his right foot and the woman with her left.

● On the second beat the man steps to the right and the woman to her left. Her weight is transferred on to her right foot, preparing to make the clockwise spin back to the starting position.

● On the third beat the woman spins back in a clockwise direction, and the man pulls her around, holding her hand at waist level.

● On the fourth beat the spin is completed and the dancers end up, feet together, in the starting position, facing each other and holding each other with their right hands.

rolling in, rolling out

These steps are found in a number of Latin American dances and are part of its attraction.

The woman appears to entwine herself in her partner's arms, only to reverse the moves and

end up standing apart. The sequence has much in common with some steps of the jive.

● The couple stand holding each with both hands. The man holds his partner with his two index fingers between the woman's thumb and index finger. At this stage of the dance they are some distance apart.

● The tap is danced on the first beat of the music; the woman taps with her right foot, and the man with his left.

● On the second beat the woman steps to the right, and the man follows her to his left. He raises his left hand above his shoulder, and then pushes her to the left, all the while continuing to hold her with his right hand.

● On the third beat the woman spins counterclockwise on her left foot, rolling in under his left arm. On the last beat the dancers come side by side, holding hands, with the man's right arm around the woman's waist.

● On the first beat of the next bar, the man taps with his right foot, and the woman with her left.

● On the second beat the couple step back. They maintain the same handhold over the first two beats of this bar, remaining side by side.

● On the third beat the man raises his left arm, and the woman rolls out, spinning clockwise on her right foot. The man pulls his partner round with his right hand, and at the same time holds her steady with his left.

● The spin takes places on one beat and has to be performed quickly. On the last beat the dancers return to their original position, and stand opposite each other, holding hands.

beat, tap ▶ beat, step ▶ beat, step ▶ beat, together ‖

merengue

on the spot

merengue—basics

Merengue is the national dance of the Dominican Republic and today has found its way all around the Caribbean and Latin America. It is a simple dance with easy movements. It can be danced by anyone, even if they have no previous experience. It is based on a two beat rhythm, in which the dancers transfer their weight from one foot to the other.

● Stand with your weight evenly on both feet with your hands at waist level. The dance relies on exaggerated hip movements by the dancers. The upper body stays still and relaxed.

● In this basic movement, dancers remain on the same position on the dance floor, changing their weight from foot to foot.

● On the first beat the dancer lifts her left leg, transferring her weight to the right. The right hip is thrust out to the side, giving the merengue its traditional look.

● On the second beat dancers carry out the same routine in reverse. The movement between the beats is quite smooth and the transition is made without stress.

● The weight has been transferred out to the left, and the dancer lifts her right floor slightly. Concentrate on the hip movement. This is more important that the movement of the feet, which move very little.

● The right hip has been thrown out to the side. In this basic move dancers remain on one spot. The movement is repeated continuously in the same position.

● The basic two beat cycle has finished and the dancer is back in her original position with her weight evenly balanced. This simple movement is at the heart of all merengue dancing.

travelling

merengue—basics

The simplicity of merengue provides many opportunities to experiment and create your own steps. This is the travelling step, back and forward: all the basic steps are the same for men and women.

● The first step is with the right leg with the weight on the left leg and the hip thrust out. On the next step, the weight shifts across to the right, so the walk assumes a swaying motion: one beat to each step.

● The first step finishes and the second step starts. Beginners should resist the temptation to turn the movement into a march. It is smoother and more seductive.

● The second step is with the right leg with the weight on the left hip. This completes the forward sequence, and the dancers immediately move backward. Note the feet are not brought together.

■ ▶ **beat, step** ▶ **beat, step** ▶ **beat, step** ▶

● Try to get the correct swaying motion going. As the step ends, the dancers start to move back. Keep your weight on the left hip and move back with the right leg. Don't change legs on the first backward movement.

● The backward steps follow the same pattern as the forward moves, but in reverse. At the next beat the first back step finishes and the weight is transferred across to the right hip.

● The dancer now steps back with his left leg, and the forward and back sequence comes to a finish.

● The dancer is now back in the starting position with his weight on the right hip, and left foot slightly in front

beat, step   ▶   **beat, step**   ▶   **beat, step**   ▶   **beat, step**   ‖

shuffling merengue—basics

This step is done the opposite way by the man and the woman.

● This is a forward and back shuffle that can be repeated continuously. Men and women dance it on opposite legs, and the step goes: forward, beat, back, beat, with the beat acting as a pause, ending on the same spot.

● The first movement of the shuffle is forward, the man steps forward with his right foot, the woman with her left. The hips follow the step out to the side.

● On the next beat the dancers transfer their weight back, the man to his left foot, the woman to her right.

● On the next beat the dancers shuffle backward, the man with his right leg, the woman with her left.

beat, shuffle ▶ **beat** ▶ **beat, shuffle** ▶

● The dancers always move one leg, and the second beat of the music is when their weight is transferred back, before the return shuffle. The man always moves his right leg, the woman her left.

● As with all merengue dancing it is important to remember the two beats of the bar. Merengue is a street dance, and relies for its appeal on its constant rhythm, as the dancers build up momentum.

● The dancers have completed their back shuffle and are coming forward again. This type of step can be repeated over and over again.

● This sequence shows three steps. Here the dancers are coming forward again, repeating step 1.

beat　　　▶　　　**beat, shuffle**　　　▶　　　**beat**　　　▶　　　**beat, shuffle**　　　Ⅱ

stepping from side to side

merengua basics

This is another simple merengue step that is danced in the same way by both men and women. It follows the two beat rhythm of the music, step, beat, step, beat, from side to side.

● Keep the hands at waist level when moving. The first step is made to the left with the weight on the right foot. Keep the step small, and allow your hips to sway out to the left as the step is completed.

● The feet should touch the floor in time with the beat of the music. As you become more proficient this becomes easier and easier.

● On the second beat the dancer brings her feet together. This sequence illustrates two steps, the first to the left, and then back to the right.

● The dancer steps to the right. See how her weight comes across from one foot to the other during the course of the beat.

● The transfer of weight is best seen by the changing position of the dancer's hips. Women should dance the merengue with their weight on the front part of the foot, making the movement easy and lively.

● On the second beat the dancer brings her feet together. It would be normal to repeat this routine a number of times before moving on to another step.

● These steps should be danced in exactly the same way by men and women. The basic rhythm is step, beat, step, beat, with the feet coming together on the beat.

travelling side to side *basics*

The merengue can be developed in a number of ways and the simplicity of the basic steps allows the dancers to strut their stuff up and down the dance floor. Some dancers walk several steps in each direction, swaying with the beat and swinging around when they want to change direction.

● Start in the normal position with your hands level with your waist and you weight on your right foot. On the first beat step back, keeping the steps short and in time with your partner. Dancers should sway down to the floor.

● The next step is taken on the second beat. Here the weight of the dancer is on his left leg and hip.

● At the end of the walk the dancer turns to the right, pivoting on his right foot. The turn is made in two movements with the feet coming together in the middle and the weight is then transferred out to the right.

● The turn takes place in two halves, with the dancers turning 90° each time. The first step back is the second part of the turn and is taken with the right leg with the weight on the left hip.

● The dancer takes a second step with his left leg to complete the sequence as shown.

● The second step has been completed and the dancer turns through 90° to face the front.

● He is now back in the starting position with his weight evenly balanced on both feet, ready to carry on to the next sequence.

the turnengue—basics

Turns are an important part of many merengue routines and are emphasised by the two beat rhythm of the music. Each 360° turn takes one bar of music to complete with half on the first beat, half on the second. It becomes an aggressive movement that can be accentuated by the swaying of the dancers as they change weight and position.

● The starting position for the 360° turn is with your feet apart, with your weight on the right leg, hip thrust out to the side. On the first beat of the music transfer your weight across to the left and swing into the turn.

● Pick up your right foot and bring it round. Put your foot down behind your left foot. At this point in the turn you have revolved about 180°.

● On the second beat transfer your weight across to your right leg and pick up your left. Swing backwards with your left leg to complete the turn. At the end of the turn transfer your weight to your left leg.

● The turn is then repeated in the opposite direction. This time, on the first beat, transfer your weight to your right leg and swing round with your left.

● You will need to keep your weight on the ball of your right foot and your right knee slightly flexed.

● The dancers have nearly finished the first part of the turn. It may be necessary to balance your body by lifting your arms out to the side. The urgent rhythm of the music gives added impetus to the movements.

● On the second beat of the music the dancers transfer their weight to their left, the right leg is lifted and swung round in a backwards movement. The turn is complete the weight of the dancers is on the right.

basic on the spot—*partners*

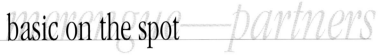

Merengue is meant to be danced with a partner. It is a close contact dance, and your partner should be held much closer than when dancing salsa. This allows the rhythm of the music to run more easily through the dancers' bodies, which will allow their movements to become synchronized.

● In all merengue dancing, the movements of the two dancers mirror each other. This sequence demonstrates the basic on the spot step shown individually on pages 56–57.

● On the first beat the man shifts his weight to the right, the woman to the left. The woman's right leg and the man's left leg bend at the knee as the weight is released.

● On the second beat the dancer's weight is shifted across to the opposite foot. Notice the pronounced sway of the hips.

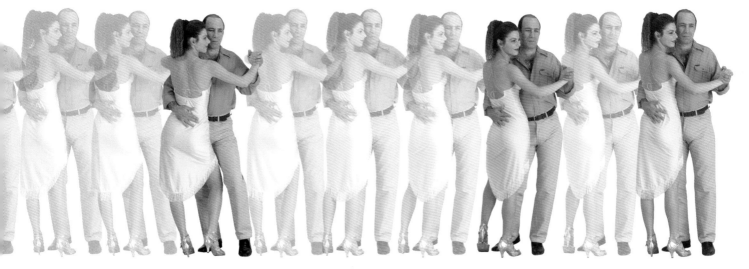

● On the next beat the weight is shifted across again. The woman's knee lifts between the man's legs so that the dancers appear to be moving as one.

● During the dance, the hands are held quite high, level with the man's shoulders. This helps to add style and precision to the dance.

● On the next beat the dancers transfer their weight back again, the woman to her right and the man to his left. This is the opening movement that is the prelude to all the merengue variations and moves.

● The music stops and the sequence— right, left, right, left— comes to an end. The dancers resume their starting position and the handhold drops towards the waist.

separating  merengue—partners

Up to now we have only covered those moves where the dancers are close together, moving to the rhythmic merengue beat. However, much of merengue dancing involves individual moves by the man and woman. This sequence illustrates the steps for the partners to separate at the start of these routines.

● The dancers start facing each other using the close hold as usual. The dancers feet are together.

● On the first beat the man transfers his weight to his right and the woman to her left, the opposite foot is raised slightly from the ground as shown. On the second beat the dancers transfer their weight across to the other side.

● At the same time, both dancers take a small step backward, the man with his right leg, the woman with her left. The man releases his right hand from the woman's waist.

■ ▶ **beat, change** ▶ **beat, step** ▶

● The couple extend their arms and take up a double handhold. At the same time, on the next beat of the bar, they transfer their weight to the other side. The dancers are now two paces apart.

● The dancers now resume the basic on the spot movement. They are now holding each other at arm's length.

● The rhythm of the music is now more evident. The dancers mirror each others movements in time with the music, and this gives the dance a hypnotic quality.

● The separating steps are the prelude to a number of merengue moves and should be performed with precision and flourish.

beat, extend arms   ❚❚   **beat, change**   ▶   **beat, change**   ❚❚

walking side to side — partners

This is one of the most attractive movements in merengue dancing. On the face of it, it seems no more than a simple walk from side to side, but danced to the music with feeling, rhythm, and flair, it symbolizes the different faces within a relationship.

● The dancers start facing each other, holding hands as shown. The man has his weight on his right foot, the woman on her left.

● On the first beat the man transfers his weight to his left and picks up his right foot. He then steps toward his partner, placing his right foot outside her right foot.

● At the same time the woman steps toward her partner with her weight on her right. On the next beat the dancers transfer their weight to the opposite foot and swing around, turning 90° as shown.

● On the next beat both dancers step in a clockwise direction and the turn is complete. The dancers face each other having turned through 180°.

■　▶　beat, change　▶　beat, step　▶　beat, step

● The turn is then repeated in the opposite direction. On the first beat of the bar the man steps with his left foot to the outside of his partner's left.

● The woman takes a step with her right foot to the man's left. It is important that these steps are taken in time with the music and the weight is transferred from side to side, as if the couple were dancing on the spot.

● The sequence illustrated shows the sway and movement of the dance. Both dancers complete the first step of the second turn, and the second step brings them back to the starting position facing each other.

● Notice that the dancers do not move from the original spot when carrying out these turns. The movement is in one direction, then the other—the essence of merengue dancing.

lady's turn merengue—partners

This move is reminiscent of a number of the salsa turns, but the two-beat rhythm in the merengue

bar makes the turn very different. You may need to practice this with your partner.

● Stand facing each other holding hands. The man has his weight on his right leg, the woman on her left.

● On the first beat the man raises his left hand above his head to allow the woman to turn. At the same time the dancers transfer their weight across to the opposite leg, man to the left, woman to the right.

● On the next beat the dancers transfer their weight back to the opposite leg and the woman starts to spin around on her left leg. The man lets go with his right hand and spins his partner with his left.

● The woman raises her right leg at the start of the turn. At the same time her weight tilts forward slightly so that she can spin around on the ball of her left foot.

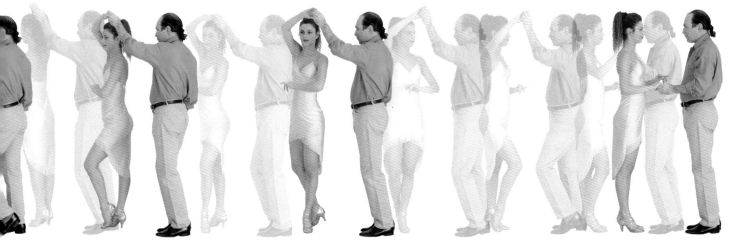

● The spin takes two beats to complete. The woman remains on her left leg throughout, but the man transfers his weight from left to right, and then back again, in time with the music.

● The turn is nearly complete. The rotation requires a certain amount of force, and the man lowers his hand slightly as it progresses, to help his partner complete the movement.

● The turn is complete and the dancers are back in the starting position, facing each other. The man has his weight on his right leg, the woman on her left.

● The woman keeps her left hand at waist level. On the last beat the couple move their feet together and resume holding hands.

beat, change ▶ ▶ beat, change beat, together II

coming together to finish and start again

This sequence shows the finish of a dance when the dancers end up together in a close hold.

● To start with, the dancers stand facing each other with the man holding his partner's right hand with his left hand only. The grip is light.

● On the first beat the dancers transfer their weight and raise their legs before stepping back, the man with his right leg, and the woman mirroring him with her left.

● The dancers move apart. Both dancers extend their arms. This is now the only point of contact between them.

● On the next beat of the music the dancers transfer their weight on to their back legs. The woman's hip is thrown out to the left and the man's to his right. The free arms should be bent with the hands at waist level.

■ ▶ beat, change ▶ beat, step ▶ beat, change ▶

● On the next beat the dancers transfer their weight back on to their front feet, as shown, and come together. The woman raises her left arm and places her hand on her partner's shoulder.

● The man places his right arm around his partner's waist, drawing her toward him.

● As the step forward is completed by the couple, the man places his right knee between his partner's legs while the woman's left leg moves outside her partner's right.

● On the next beat the dancers transfer their weight to the opposite side, and the woman lifts her right leg so that it is between her partner's. The sequence finishes with the couple in the close contact hold.

beat, step forward ▶ ▶ **beat, together** ▶ **beat, together** **II**

rolling in, rolling out *partners*

This is an exciting variation that adds lots of movement to the dance. At the same time, it is important to maintain the basic merengue rhythm: this can easily get lost in the complications of the movement. Check the sequence carefully before putting it into practice.

● Start facing your partner, the man holding the woman's left hand in his right. On the first beat the dancers start the basic merengue rhythm, man to the right while the woman steps left toward her partner.

● On the next beat the woman spins on her left leg through 180°, maintaining the handhold and moving in toward her partner so that they end up side by side as shown.

● On the next beat the dancers move back, the man changing his weight on to his right leg and then swinging around. The woman also pivots on her right leg. The handhold remains the same.

● On the next beat the man transfers his weight to his left side and the woman follows him, transferring her weight across to the left.

| ■ | **beat, change** | ▶ | **beat, spin** | ▶ | **beat, back** | ▶ | **beat, change** | ▶ |

● The whole movement is carried out in a series of steps with the man "walking" around the outside. The woman steps backward and pivots, keeping level with her partner with her left arm across her body.

● The couple have now turned through 360°. On the next beat the man transfers his weight to his left and the woman starts to roll out through 360°, pivoting on her left foot.

● Notice how the dancers maintain the merengue step and style, changing weight on each beat of the music. This gives the rolling turn a rhythmic, rocking look.

● The last turn has been completed and the couple are back in their starting position. This move requires some practice to perfect.

side step as partners

merengue partners

Merengue is the dance of the Caribbean islands and the Dominican Republic. In the 20th century it was transformed from a native dance to a popular dance in ballrooms and dance clubs.

● This sequence illustrates the side step with a partner. This is one of the ballroom moves that was adopted by merengue at the beginning of the 20th century when ballroom dancing became popular.

● Start in the close contact hold. On the first beat of the music the man transfers his weight to his right, the woman to her left.

● On the second beat, as the dancers transfer their weight on to their other foot, the man steps out to the side as shown. The girl steps to her left and the couple pivot around 90°.

● The couple then step again on the next beat, when the dancers transfer their weight to the left and right respectively. On the following beat the man steps left again, and the woman turns around on the same spot.

■ ▶ **beat, change** ▶ **beat, step** ▶ **beat, step, beat, step** ▶

● Again the dancers change weight on the beat, and on the following beat, they move round again to the left. The man in effect walks around his partner on each beat of the music, the woman turning with him.

● The movement carries the dancers through 180°. When the first turn has been completed they then reverse, side stepping back in the opposite direction.

● The turn can be danced to suit the partners, either vigorously, around and then back, or more slowly, with each turn taking a number of steps to complete.

● The sequence has finished and the dancers face each other. Note how the close contact hold is maintained throughout, giving the impression that the two dancers are moving as one.

woman steps around the man

This is another teasing movement of merengue where the woman walks around her partner and then returns to him. The man stays facing in the same direction, waiting for her to come back.

● The dancers face each other with a single handhold, the man holding the woman's right hand in his left.

● On the first beat the man takes a travelling step forward, pulling his hand to the left and passing his right arm over his partner's left shoulder. The woman steps to her left and releases her hold with her right hand.

● On the next beat the man moves the woman behind him: she then steps around behind her partner with her weight on her left leg.

● The man takes a pace to his left, and the woman completes her turn behind her partner, and then tucks her right hand under his left arm as shown. The man faces in the original direction, the woman has turned 180°.

● On the next beat the man pulls the woman in front of him, and she starts to dance and turn around again. The man's left hand moves up to the woman's right shoulder, moving her though 180°.

● On the next beat the turn is completed. The dancers come around, facing one another, holding right to left in a single handhold.

● They then dance the sequence shown on pages 76–77 to finish the routine. On the first beat they transfer their weight back to their front feet, and the woman puts her hand around her partner's neck.

● The man draws the woman toward him with his hand around her waist, and they step together into the close contact hold to complete the routine.

the cuddle
merengue—partners

The cuddle is another of those intricate merengue moves that adds such spice to the dance.
The effect on the floor is of the girl rolling around the man, who turns away and then turns back
at the end of the movement.

● The dancers start facing each other holding hands in the normal way. On the first beat they shift their weight to left and right respectively, and the man lifts his right hand leading the woman behind him.

● On the next beat, as the weight is transferred to the other foot the woman steps behind the man, who brings his right arm across the left with the woman's arm passing over his head.

● The next beat carries the woman round behind the man. He faces the front and the couple hold hands with the man's hands crossed, his left arm at waist level and his right at shoulder level as shown.

● On the next beat the man starts to turn away, clockwise, with the woman following him, using the travelling step.

■ **beat, arm up** ▶ **beat, behind, beat, over** ▶ **beat, behind** ▶ **beat, man turns** ▶

● This move can continue around and around for as long as the dancers wish. To bring the movement to an end, the man extends his right arm, the woman lets go with her right arm, and she steps around to the front.

● This move takes three beats, and the couple end up facing each other in a single handhold.

● The couple then dance a lady's turn, shown on pages 74–75 to finish. In this sequence the woman turns clockwise under the man's left arm.

● On the next beat the couple are back facing each other, holding hands as shown above. This is one of the most popular of the merengue moves.

beat, extend　　‖　▶　**beat, turn**　　▶ **beat, face**　　‖

shoulder roll

The shoulder roll has much in common with the cuddle shown on pages 84–85 but the movement is looser and the dancers further apart. The steps are very much in the style of the ballroom, and this move can be traced directly to the second half of the 20th century when ballroom dancing became popular and merengue adopted a number of the steps.

● The dancers start facing each other with their hands crossed, right hand to right hand, with the left hands underneath.

● The dancers sway right and left on the first beat, and on the second beat the woman turns clockwise with both hands passing over her head as she revolves.

● On the next beat the woman continues her turn. At this point the man passes his left arm over his head so that the woman's left arm lies across the back of his shoulders. The woman has turned through 360°.

● On the next beat the couple sway apart and step to the side, the woman going behind the man. The right hands are also raised above shoulder height, which gives the move its name of shoulder roll.

■ **beat, right** ▶   **beat, turn** ▶   **beat, turn, across** ▶   ‖ **beat, across** ▶

● The dancers take a second step sideways, travelling in opposite directions. The woman has moved from the man's right to the left. The man's left arm is now extended across his partner's chest.

● The couple then lift their right arms and bring them back over the man's head, facing each other in the cross handhold.

● To finish the move the woman spins clockwise, passing underneath the couple's right hands, turning through 360°. The couple continue to hold hands during this spin.

● The turn is completed with the woman passing under their left arms. The couple come face to face and resume the normal handhold before starting the next routine.

beat, step　　　Ⅱ　　　**beat, lift arms**　　　▶　　　**beat, spin**　　　▶　　　**beat, face**　　　Ⅱ

the spring

merengue—partners

The spring is an exotic merengue move where the dancers come together into close contact and
then move apart. This is emphasized by the movement of the dancers' arms.

● The dancers stand facing each
other holding hands. On the first beat
the dancers transfer their weight, the
man to his right and the woman to
her left.

● On the next beat the dancers step
backward, arms extended. The hands
are dropped to waist level.

● On the next beat the dancers
transfer their weight back to their
front legs and step forward. The man
raises his arms to chest height and
pulls the woman toward him.

● On the next beat the dancers step
together, raising their arms above their
heads. The man's right knee goes
between the woman's legs, and on the
next beat the woman's right knee
goes between the man's legs.

■ **beat, transfer** ▶ **beat, back** ▶ **beat, forwards** ▶ **beat, up** **11**

● On the next beat the dancers move apart and lower their hands, repeating the routine. This can be done as many times as the dancers wish.

● The dancers are now two steps apart with their arms extended. To finish the routine the man throws the woman's arms into the air but lets go with both hands.

● As the couple step together, the man's puts his right hand around his partner's waist and holds his left hand out to the side. The woman drops her right hand into her partner's left and they take up the close contact hold.

● On the last beat the dancers move apart and stand facing each other, holding each other in the normal handhold.

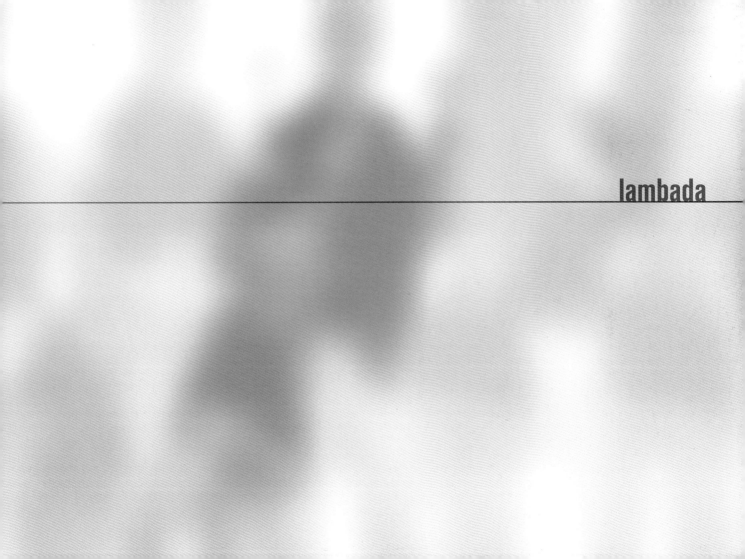

lambada

step forward and back basics

In lambada there are three beats to the bar with a "quick, quick, slow" rhythm. The first beat is usually on the spot, with the following movements forward and back.

● Unlike salsa and merengue, the lambada is danced with the whole body, emphasized by the woman's swaying head movements. On the first beat the dancers step forward with their left feet, their hips follow to the left.

● The second quick beat is another forward step, this time with the right foot with the right hip swaying out. The arms are held at waist level. The step is completed and dancers now move backward with their left feet.

● This time the beat and movement are slow. The sensuous movements of the lambada are emphasized by the swaying steps of the dancers and the arms movements which add to this.

■ **quick, step** ▶ **quick, step** ▶ **slow, step back** ‖

● The lambada used to be known as the "forbidden dance". It sprang from a variety of Latin American dances and takes its name from the lambaterias, the small bars and cafés where people danced.

● The next step is a small backward movement with the right foot. The beat is quick. Women always dance the lambada on their toes with their knees slightly bent throughout the dance, the men on the whole foot.

● The dancers move back again, this time on their left feet. The hip movement follows this out to the left. This is the opposite of merengue where the leg and hip movements go in opposite directions.

● Dancers then step forward to finish the basic movement on the slow beat. Beginners should practice these steps until they have mastered the rhythm of the dance.

on the spot
lambada—basics

Although the lambada is a dance of movement and rhythm, the basic steps are simple. It is important to master the basic lambada routine, dancing on the spot, when the dancers can start to fuse their bodies into the routine using these moves as a prelude to the climax of the dance.

● On the first beat the dancers transfer their weight to their right side with the hip going out to the right.

● On the second beat of the bar, the weight comes back and the hips go across. This helps the dancers to create a pronounced side to side movement, one after the other, in quick succession.

● Note that in this basic sequence the dancers stay on the same spot throughout. The rhythm is built up entirely by the changing weight and movement of the dancers' hips and bodies.

● On the third beat in the bar the dancers slow. They lift their right knees and the transfer of weight is done far more deliberately.

● This basic routine is then repeated the other way around. This time the first transfer is to the left.

● The normal dress for lambada is short skirts for the women and tight trousers for the men. These help to show the movements to their best advantage.

● On the second quick beat of the music, the dancers transfer back to their right side. This is followed by the slow movement, this time back to the left. Notice the pronounced knee lift the dancers use for this.

● The sequence come to an end and the dancers are back in their starting position with their weight on their right feet.

side step

lambada—basics

There is a good deal of side to side movement when dancing the lambada in the same way as salsa and merengue. This is incorporated into the rhythm of the dance. The three beats to the bar of all lambada music is ideal for this and provides both impetus and interest.

● Start on the quick beat with the weight on your left foot. Point your toes slightly outward. The left hip should be out to the left as normal.

● Lift your right foot and step to the right. Keep your left heel out to the right but move your right hip out in the direction you are moving as the step progresses.

● The step to the right has been completed. The right hip is thrown out to the side, as can be seen above. Bring your right shoulder forward during this step so that your body makes a quarter turn toward the left.

● The arms follow the step, this develops into the slow beat when the dancers move back to the left. The movement is deliberate while the dancers return to their starting position, facing the front.

● The side step is then repeated in reverse. This time dancers transfer their weight on to their right feet on the first beat of the bar.

● On the second beat, dancers step to the left. The left foot is raised with the right heel pointing to the left.

● Dancers then take a step back to the right on the slow beat. See how the body is turned in the direction of the step, keeping the hips well out to the left. This gives the lambada its sensuous look.

● The second sequence has been completed and the dancer is facing the front. The sequence shows the flexible knee position necessary to perform this dance with true style.

opening up ~~lambada—basics~~

This sequence shows the basic opening up steps where dancers change from travelling in one direction to another. The sequence shows the essential difference between the lambada and salsa and merengue. The posture of the dancer is much looser, bodies should be flexible and supple, and the whole feel of the dance is livelier.

● To start, stand with your weight on both feet, knees slightly bent, with your left foot in front. On the first beat of the bar, turn your left foot to the right and transfer your weight to the left with your hip thrown out to the left.

● On the next beat step back with your right foot and transfer your weight across, thrusting out your right hip to the right. Turn away slightly as you carry out this movement as if your body was following your foot.

● On the third beat move your weight back on to your left foot, and bring your right foot around, so that you are, again, facing the front.

■ ▶ **quick, weight left** ▶ **quick, step back** ▶ **slow, together** II

● This sequence is then repeated on the other side. On the first quick beat of the bar turn your left foot to the right, and then transfer your weight to the right with your right hip moving out to the side.

● On the second beat step back with your left foot, with your weight out to the left. Your body turns through the best part of 90° during this movement as shown.

● On the slow beat your right foot comes back around your left and your weight changes across to your left.

● As shown above, the dancers pivot on their right feet in this movement and end up facing the front, weight on the right, with their right hips out to the side.

woman's head roll—*basics*

The essence of lambada is that the girl follows the man and is "as putty in his hands." One of the ways that girls can show their independence is by decorating the dance with head rolls.

● The steps of this routine follow the opening up movements shown on pages 96–97. On the first beat the weight comes on to the left leg with the left hip thrust out to the side. The dancer turns slightly to the right.

● On the second beat the right foot steps behind, and the dancer's body swings through 180°. The weight is on the right foot with the right hip out. The dancer's head leans over her right shoulder.

● On the slow beat the dancer transfers her weight on to her left foot and drops her head forward as shown. She turns her body away and brings her feet together facing away.

● The dancer's head stays in the forward position. On the next beat her weight goes to the right, and then back to the left, as she takes a step back, at the same time swinging her head around.

■ **quick, weight left**   ▶   **quick, step back**   ▶   **slow, head down**   ▶   **quick, quick, head roll**   ▶

● On the slow beat she returns to the starting position but with her head still down. The sequence is then repeated on the other side. Quick beat, weight to the left.

● On the second quick beat the dancer steps back with her right leg, swinging her body around, rolling her head from right to left. The speed of the music adds momentum and drama to this.

● Notice the position of her hips as this movement is carried out. On the slow beat the dancer transfers her weight over to the left with her left hip out, and brings her head upright.

● The sequence is complete and the dancer has returned to her starting position with her weight on her right leg.

slow, head down, quick ‖ **quick, step back, head roll** ▶ **slow, head up** ‖

the turn lambada—basics

The Lambada comes from Brazil. There the dance originated and developed, although the exact origins are unclear. It has become increasingly popular in Europe and the rest of the world over the last twenty years. The basic turn or spin is one of the innovative moves it has developed in that time.

● When dancing the lambada, the turn is easily performed. This sequence shows two complete turns, the first counterclockwise, the second clockwise. As with all lambada moves, they can be danced either way.

● On the first quick beat the dancer transfers his weight to the left, left hip out. On the second beat he takes a small step across to the right.

● The step to the right has been completed and the weight is on the right hip. On the slow beat, dancers should drop their right shoulders and use the momentum to spin around in a 360° turn as shown.

● The turn has to be completed before the first beat of the next bar. Dancers spin around on the balls of their left feet.

● The counterclockwise spin has been completed and the sequence can now be repeated, this time spinning in a clockwise direction

● On the first quick beat, the weight is transferred to the right with the right hip out. On the second beat the dancer takes a small step back to the left, and at the same time drops his left shoulder.

● The third beat sees the start of the spin. This time dancers will pivot on their right feet turning in a clockwise direction.

● The spin has now been completed and the dancer is back in the starting position facing the front. Many of the moves in the lambada incorporate this spin in various forms.

the step over

lambada—basics

Another influence on the development of the lambada was the music of the Caribbean. The steel drums and electric guitars added their unique musical experience to the lambada rhythms. There are also traces of old Spanish dances, and flamenco accents can be seen in a number of the moves. In the basic step over, where the dancers sway backward, shows some influence.

● Start with your weight on the right foot, hip out to the side. On the first beat take a step with your left leg across in front of your right. This step should be as large as possible. Hold your arms out for balance.

● With hips moving forward, dancers sway back, arching their backs as far as possible. This is the character of the dance. On the second quick beat the right foot comes together with the left. On the third slow beat transfer your weight on to your left leg.

● At the same time make a turn to the left through 180° to face the opposite direction. The sequence is now repeated facing the other way. The first step on the first quick beat is made with the right leg.

● Again, make the step as large as possible and sway back as your hips come forward. The impetus of the step helps you to keep your balance.

● The further back you can bend, the more energy there is in the dance. Hold your arms out to help you to maintain your balance.

● On the second quick beat the legs come together as before. As you transfer your weight across to the right, the slow beat of the bar is the signal to start the turn. This time the turn is to the right.

● All dancers will find it a help if they drop their shoulders slightly as they start the turn. The impetus then carries them around the 180°, back to their starting position.

forward and back—*partners*

In the lambada, the man leads and the woman follows. The couple should move as one.

● In the lambada the partners dance very close together, with the man leading the woman. Their movements mirror each other. The basic forward and back movement follows the sequence shown on pages 92–93.

● On the first quick beat the man takes a small step forward with his left foot, his hip out to the left. On the second beat he steps forward with his right leg. His knee goes between the woman's legs.

● On the third slow beat the dancers return to their original position, the man stepping back with his left leg and the woman forward. The woman's right knee goes between the man's legs as shown.

● The dancers have returned to their original position. The routine is then repeated in reverse, this time the woman advances and the man retires.

quick, step, quick, step ▶ **slow, return**

● The man takes a small step back with his right leg while the woman steps forward with her left. On the second quick beat the man steps back with his left leg, transferring his weight to the left.

● The woman mirrors his movements. The third slow beat of the music has arrived; the man steps forward with his right leg, knee bent and hip out to the right. The woman moves back in harmony.

● The step ends and the couple have returned to their original position. The close contact hold and hand position does not change during this basic routine.

● For a successful partnership in lambada, the dancers must move as one. The movement is started by the man pushing his leg against his partner's while she responds to his moves.

▶ **quick, step, quick, step**   ▶ **slow**

man side step, woman opening up

This routine provides the woman with an opportunity to decorate the movement with the head roll demonstrated on pages 100–101. The dancers open up for this move.

● The dancers start in the close contact hold. On the first beat the man lowers his left hand toward the woman's right hip and pushes her away.

● The man steps away to the left and the woman steps to the right, both dancers transferring their weight out to the side as shown. The woman leans her head over her right shoulder, preparing for the head roll.

● On the second beat the man moves across to his right, the woman side steps to his front rolling her head from right to left.

● The woman's weight is now on her right leg, the head roll is finished. The man pulls her toward him into an upright position. On the slow beat the movement is completed. The man steps to his right turning through 90°.

● The couple now repeat the movement. On the first beat the man steps back with his right leg, while the woman side steps to her left. Her head moves over her left shoulder.

● On the second beat the man moves back on to his left leg, pulling the woman to the left in front of him. The woman is now in front of the man, head down, rolling her head from left to right.

● On the third beat the turn and head roll are both completed; the man steps to his left while the woman steps back on to her right leg.

● As the couple move apart, the man holds out his arms with his right hand, coming to the woman's hip. Repeat these steps as many times as you wish.

sideways dip

lambada—partners

The sideways dip is a favorite lambada move and follows on from the moves on pages 108–109.

● This is an acrobatic move that needs to be practiced before it is performed in public. The move starts on the second quick beat: the woman's weight is on her right leg, the man stands with his legs wide apart.

● The man holds the woman with his right hand, the woman holds the man's left arm while he pulls her towards him. On the third slow beat the couple move together as shown. The woman prepares to turn.

● The woman finishes her turn through 180° and bends backward into the dip. Her weight should be on her toes with her left leg in front of her right. The turn and dip down are on the two quick beats of the bar.

● The dancers go down into the dip and up on the slow beat. It is important that both dancers maintain a firm grip during this move.

● The man lowers his left arm to allow his partner to drop to the horizontal position. He bends his knees but keeps his upper body straight as shown.

● On the slow beat the dancers return to the upright position. The whole movement should appear smooth and effortless. At the end of the beat the couple are upright and the next bar of music starts.

● On the first beat the man and woman transfer their weight to the right. On the second beat the dancers take a step sideways and to the left. This brings them around facing one another.

● On this beat of the bar the dancers move apart. The woman transfers her weight to her right, and the man to his right, ready to continue dancing.

slow, up　　　　　**‖**　　　　　**▶**　　　　**quick, transfer, quick, step**　　**▶**　　**slow, apart**　　　　　**‖**

back dip

This is another acrobatic move that carries straight on from pages 110–111. The move needs to be practiced: women should only dip backward as far back as they feel comfortable.

● The move is shown from the second quick beat; the man has his weight on his left foot, the woman on the right. The dancers do an on-the-spot move on this beat; man to the left, and woman to the right.

● On the slow beat the woman moves back on to her right foot, and the man moves back on to his left. The man stays in position while the woman turns counterclockwise.

● The man releases his partner's hand and slides his hand around his partner's waist as she comes towards him, at the same time taking her right hand in his left.

● On the first quick beat the couple come together in a close hold. The woman grips her partner's right leg between her knees. His right arm is around her waist.

● On the next beat the woman sways back with her weight on her toes, dipping down away from her partner. The man transfers his weight forward on to his right foot.

● As his partner dips backward the man leans forward, holding his partner by the waist, with his left hand holding her right. The woman grips her partner's right leg with her knees to help her maintain her balance.

● The rise from the dip is very slow and danced over a complete bar of music. The change in tempo contributes to the exotic feel of the dance.

● As the movement finishes, the man steps forward on to his left leg while the woman stands on her toes. The couple take up a close contact hold.

turning the woman

This is a simple routine that has much in common with some of the spins of the jive, where the girl turns backward and forward under her partner's arm. The quick, quick, slow rhythm of the lambada gives a unique feel to these movements. The man performs the basic on the spot steps during the turns, holding the woman's right hand up with his left hand so that the woman turns underneath.

● The dancers start holding each other at arm's length as shown. The first quick beat of the bar is danced on the spot, the man to his right, and the woman to her left.

● On the next beat the man steps to the side, to his left, and the woman follows him, stepping to her right. The hips of both dancers move across in the normal lambada style.

● On the slow beat of the bar the man moves back to the right and raises his left hand, the woman starts to spin under his arm, turning in a counterclockwise direction, spinning on the ball of her left foot.

● The man leads the woman around the 360° spin. As she comes facing him, the dancers step right and left on the first beat on the next bar.

■ ▶ **quick, step** ▶ **quick, step** ▶ **slow, turn** ▶ **quick, step** ▶

● On the second beat, the man steps sideways to the right, and the woman to the left. The man raises his left arm as in the previous turn.

● On the slow beat the woman spins in a clockwise direction, balancing on the ball of her right foot. Remember that women should always be on their toes when doing the lambada. This adds to the charm of the dance.

● As the turn comes to an end, the man lowers his left arm and holds out his right hand. The couple face each other, holding hands at waist level, at the end of the beat.

● The dancers are now ready to continue with other movements. You can either build up a regular lambada routine or dance spontaneously, performing whatever moves you wish at the time.

figure of eight — partners

This is another lambada move that has much in common with jiving. It is quite complicated to do satisfactorily, and it is a help when the couple know the routine inside out. The main problems come with the direction of the turns, with the dancer's arms passing over their heads in various directions.

● Start holding hands in the normal way, facing each other. On the first beat the man takes a large step forward with his right foot across the front of the woman, and the woman does the same with her left.

● The man's right foot is in front of the woman's right foot so, in effect, she is now standing behind him. The man raises his right arm above his own head.

● On the second beat the couple transfer their weight on to the other foot and turn clockwise through 180°. As the turn progresses, the man lets go with his left hand and then catches the woman's hand on the other side.

● On the slow beat the couple transfer their weight, standing opposite each other. The man moves from left to right, and the woman from right to left.

● The turn is then repeated in the opposite direction. This time the woman steps forward with her right foot, placing it in front of her partner's right foot. The man steps behind her, and the woman turns to the front.

● On the next beat the turn starts, again rotating clockwise. The woman's right arm is pulled over her head and across her shoulders. The couple let go with their right and left hands.

● As they come face to face, the dancers take up their normal handhold. On the slow beat they transfer their weight; this time the man moves from right to left, and the woman from left to right.

● The figure of eight is now completed. This can then be repeated as often as you wish or the dancers can move on to the next routine.

▶ **quick, step**　　　▶ **quick, turn**　　　▶ **slow, transfer**　　　**11**

rolling in, rolling out *partners*

This is another routine that has much in common with jiving. It is a lot of fun to dance with the woman rolling in toward the man and then rolling away again. The beat of lambada music adds life to this move, as do the varying rhythms.

● The couple hold each other with a single handhold, with the man's right hand in his partner's left. On the first beat the man steps to his right and the woman to her left, dancing on the spot in the normal way.

● On the second beat of the bar the man moves back to his left, and the woman to her right. The couple are now some distance apart, with their weight away from each other.

● On the third slow beat, the man transfers his weight back to his right and the woman spins forward in a counterclockwise direction.

● The woman spins on her left foot, rolling herself inside her partner's right arm. At the end of this beat the woman has turned through 180° and the couple are side by side, standing close together.

▶ **quick, step** ▶ **quick, step** ▶ **quick, turn** ▶

● The rolling out movement is the same in reverse. On the first beat the woman transfers her weight to her right leg, and the man to his left. This movement is a small one, danced on the spot.

● The couple continue to hold each other with the man's arm around the woman's waist. On the second beat the woman steps back with her left foot, and the man forward with his right.

● On the third beat, as the man moves back on to his left foot, the woman moves forward and rolls out, spinning clockwise on her right foot.

● The spin is complete and the dancers are back facing one another. They are in a position to dance this routine again or proceed to another variation.

side lean

The side lean is another of those acrobatic moves of lambada that can be performed by all dancers supple and daring enough. It follows on from the sequence on pages 118–119. Like many of these moves, it is better to practice this first before you try this out on the dance floor.

● The dance follows the the roll in, roll out move with the side lean as an addition. The couple face each other, holding hands. On the first beat the man moves on to his right foot, and the woman to her left.

● On the second beat the couple step back—the man on to his left foot, and the woman onto her right. The couple are now some distance apart.

● On the slow beat the woman rolls towards her partner, turning in a counterclockwise direction. The man stays in the same position with his feet apart.

● As the couple come together, the woman raises her right knee and leans against her partner with her left hip. The man puts his left hand on his partner's elbow for additional support.

▪ ▶ **quick, step** ▶ **quick, step** ▶ **slow, roll in, lean**

● On the first beat of the next bar the man bends his left knee, keeping his shoulders and upper body straight. The woman leans over, following her partner as he moves away from her. Her right arm is raised by her head.

● On the second beat the man straightens his knee, transferring his weight back to his right leg. The couple rise together.

● On the third beat the couple roll out as shown on pages 118–9. The woman spins around in a clockwise direction, turning on her right leg. The man pulls her around, unwinding his arm round her waist.

● The move is finished and the couple are back facing each other holding hands as shown.

side dip
lambada—partners

This as another spectacular move that requires practice and perfect timing to bring off. One of the important things to remember when performing any dips is that these should start as a wave moving upward from the knees via the hips, waist, and shoulders with the head movement the last of all. They are moves for the physically fit, one of the great attractions of lambada.

● Start facing each other holding hands. This allows the dip to be lower. If you do not want to dip so far, the man can hold his partner around her waist. On the first beat the couple dance right and left on the spot.

● On the second beat the couple step back. The man takes a large step sideways on to his left foot, and the woman steps back on to her right. The dancers transfer their weight out as shown.

● On the third beat the man remains in the same position, and the woman transfers her weight on to the ball of her left foot.

● The woman completes her turn through 180°, placing her right foot behind her left. The dancers finish the turn, the man standing sideways on. The dancers hold their arms up at shoulder height.

● On the first beat of the next bar the woman bends backwards from her knees. Her partner holds her firmly by her hands.

● Lambada experts can bend parallel with the floor as shown here. On the second beat the man pulls the woman back into an upright position.

● On the slow beat the woman spins clockwise on her right foot through 180°. The man transfers his weight on to his left foot, and the couple complete the movement facing each other.

● Energetic dancers can plan a program involving all the dips, one after the other. Only incorporate as many as you feel happy with, beginners should not be too ambitious.

around the world

This is the last lambada move that we have room for in this book. It is one of the most famous, aptly called "around the world". The movements are very quick, and it contains many of the elements that make lambada such an exciting dance, close hold, spectacular movement, startling acrobatics.

● The dancers start in the close hold facing each other. On the first beat the couple dance on the spot.

● The man moves to his right, and the woman to her left. They both transfer their weight to the side as normal.

● On the second beat the man steps back on to his left foot and the woman steps back on to her right. The dancers extend their arms but retain hold of each other.

● On the third beat the man transfers his weight on to his right foot. The woman turns to face her partner, turning on her left foot. At the end of the turn, she places her right foot between her partner's legs.

● On the first beat of the second bar, the woman continues her turn through 180°, pivoting on her right foot. The man holds her with his arm around her waist and the woman bends over backwards.

● On the second beat the woman stays in the same position and the man swivels her through 180°, back to his right. Her right leg remains between his legs as they pivot around.

● On the third beat the man pulls the woman toward him and the dancers resume the upright position in the close hold. The couple bring their feet together as shown.

● The around the world movement can then be repeated in the opposite direction. The moves are reversed in the normal way.

quick, turn ▶ **quick, swing round** ▶ **slow. together**

index